STARTI
JOU

Published by Christian Art Publishers
PO Box 1599, Vereeniging, 1930, RSA

First edition 2014

Cover designed by Christian Art Publishers

Images used under license from Shutterstock.com

Printed in China

ISBN 978-1-4321-1057-4

14 15 16 17 18 19 20 21 22 23 – 11 10 9 8 7 6 5 4 3 2

STARTING *the* JOURNEY

ANGUS BUCHAN™

CONTENTS

Dear Friend,

God loves you and cares about you. He has a special plan and purpose for your life.

God wants to start on a very special journey with you and walk beside you to lead and guide you.

I would love to tell you about God's very special plan for you in the pages that follow …

Angus Buchan.

Part 1
SALVATION

What Is Salvation?

God loves you and created you to be in a relationship with Him. God is good, loving and holy (without sin). But every one of us sins and is born with a sinful nature. We choose to do wrong and to turn our back on God. Our sin separates us from God because He is holy and cannot look upon sin. God does not want anyone to be separated from Him, but our sin has caused our relationship with Him to be broken. God has given us freedom to choose and we have chosen to do wrong.

Sin results in death and all of us deserve to die and be cut off from God forever. All of us are headed to hell which is final and eternal separation from God.

> For all have sinned and fall short of the glory of God.
> ROMANS 3:23

But because God loves us He has provided a way for us to be saved from hell and for our relationship with Him to be restored. The

Father loves you and me so much that He gave us Jesus Christ, His only Son. God sacrificed His Son for you and me when we were still sinners so that we might have everlasting life. That is love. It is so amazing.

> But God showed His great love for us by sending Christ to die for us while we were still sinners.
> ROMANS 5:8

Jesus Christ is God's only provision for man's sin. Through Him alone can we know God personally and be forgiven for our sins.

> *For Christ also suffered once for sins, the just for the unjust, that He might bring us to God.*
> *1 Peter 3:18*

> *Christ died for our sins according to the Scriptures, that He was buried, that He was raised on the third day according to the Scriptures, and that He appeared ... to more than five hundred of the brothers and sisters at the same time.*
> *1 Corinthians 15:3-6*

Jesus Christ Is the Only Way to Heaven

Some people try to bridge the gap between themselves and God by doing good works or getting involved in religious activities. But this is all in vain because it is impossible to earn salvation. Salvation is a free gift we receive through Jesus' sacrifice on the cross.

> For the wages of sin is death, but the gift of God is eternal life in Christ Jesus our Lord.
>
> ROMANS 6:23

Jesus said in John 14:6, *"I am the way, the truth, and the life. No one comes to the Father except through Me."* Since this is the case, it doesn't matter how good or religious you are, according to the Word of God you are not going to heaven. Good people don't go to heaven, believers go to heaven. Believing in whom? *Believing in Jesus Christ, the Son of the living God.*

God sent His one and only Son to the earth to live as a man. He was sinless and without fault. Then He was crucified for our sins. On the cross He took all of our sin, shame, guilt and death upon Himself and conquered it all when He rose from the dead.

Jesus suffered in our place. He was like a lamb without spot or blemish who was sacrificed on behalf of our sin. Through His death we have life and the forgiveness of sin. We can now be reconciled with God because our sins have been washed away through the blood of Christ and we have been made clean.

Through Jesus' sacrifice on the cross we can look forward to eternal life with Him!

"Nor is there salvation in any other,
for there is no other name under heaven
given among men by which
we must be saved."
Acts 4:12

"Believe on the Lord Jesus Christ,
and you will be saved."
Acts 16:31

Who Can Be Saved?

One of the most important Scripture verses in the Bible is John 3:16. This is what it says: *"For God so loved the world that He gave His only begotten Son, that whoever believes in Him should not perish but have everlasting life."* That *whoever believes in Him,* not whoever is a good person, not whoever tries his best, no, whoever believes in Him *shall not perish* – shall be saved and have eternal life.

It is so simple. It's amazing. People come to me and say, "No, it can't be that simple. There must be some catch. There must be something I've got to do."

You don't have to do anything. All you have to do is believe.

> *For it is by grace you have been saved, through faith – and this is not from yourselves, it is the gift of God – not by works, so that no one can boast.*
> *Ephesians 2:8-9*

But when the kindness and love of God our Savior appeared, He saved us, not because of righteous things we had done, but because of His mercy. He saved us through the washing of rebirth and renewal by the Holy Spirit, whom He poured out on us generously through Jesus Christ our Savior, so that, having been justified by His grace, we might become heirs having the hope of eternal life.
Titus 3:4-7

But we are all like an unclean thing, and all our righteousnesses are like filthy rags; We all fade as a leaf, and our iniquities, like the wind, have taken us away.
Isaiah 64:6

"There is none righteous, no, not one; there is none who understands; there is none who seeks after God. They have all turned aside; they have together become unprofitable; there is none who does good, no, not one."
Romans 3:10-12

A Personal Invitation

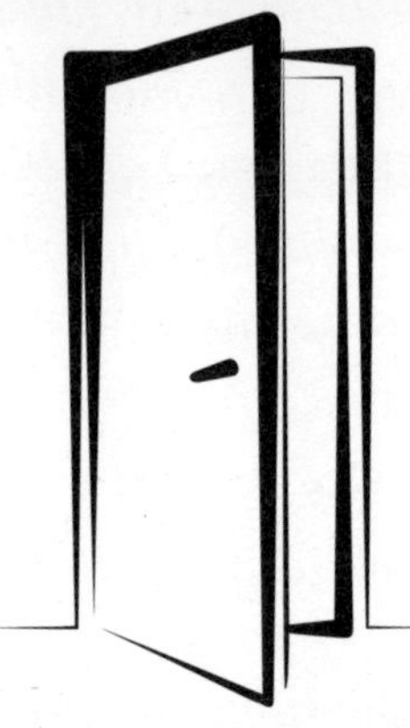

In Revelation 3:20 Jesus says: *"Behold, I stand at the door and knock. If anyone hears My voice and opens the door, I will come in to him and dine with him, and he with Me."*

In other words: "Knock, knock, knock, can you hear Me knocking at the door?" But the handle is on the inside of the door, there is no handle on the outside. So unless you open the door and Jesus comes in and dines with you and you with Him, He cannot have fellowship with you.

You have got to open the door today and say: "Lord, today I want You to come into my life.

Today is spring day, today is the first day of the rest of my life. I want to make a change in my life." It is up to you. Can you do that today? Can you say, "Lord, please give me a second chance. Lord, I have been messing up my life. Lord, I have had no peace in my life."

God has given us the freedom to choose whether to open the door and invite Him in or not.

> *"Whoever calls on the name*
> *of the Lord shall be saved."*
> *Romans 10:13*

> *If you confess with your mouth the Lord Jesus and believe in your heart that God has raised Him from the dead, you will be saved. For with the heart one believes unto righteousness, and with the mouth confession is made unto salvation.*
> *Romans 10:9-10*

Second Chances

No matter what bad decisions you might have made in the past, you always have a second chance with the Lord. Repent today and say, "Lord, please give me another chance." I promise you that if you repent of your sin and ask Him to be Lord of your life, He will cancel your sin. He came for those who are lost.

What does it mean to repent? It means to say, "Sorry, Lord. Please forgive me. I am turning around and I am walking the other way." Jesus Christ died for all of our sins. He says, "Go, your sins are forgiven."

If we confess our sins, He is faithful and just to forgive us our sins and to cleanse us from all unrighteousness.
1 John 1:9

Repent and turn to God, so that
your sins may be wiped out.
Acts 3:19

"I have blotted out, like a thick cloud, your transgressions, and like a cloud, your sins. Return to Me, for I have redeemed you."
Isaiah 44:22

As far as the east is from the west, so far has He removed our transgressions from us.
Psalm 103:12

You will perish, too, unless you repent of your sins and turn to God.
Luke 13:3

Tomorrow Might Be Too Late

You might say to yourself, "I'll think about changing my life tomorrow." My dear friend, the road that leads to hell is paved with good intentions. No more tomorrows.

If I had not asked Jesus into my heart on 18 February 1979, I can tell you I wouldn't be here today. I would have died in my sin. I was not coping. This is about you and about Jesus Christ. *"Seek first the kingdom of God and His righteousness, and all these things shall be added to you"* (Matthew 6:33).

What have I got to do? What you have to do is pray a prayer of repentance. Then turn from your wicked ways and follow Him and He will give you life abundantly. The thief comes to steal, kill and destroy. But Jesus said, *"I came that they may have life abundantly"* (John 10:10).

> *"Repent, for the kingdom of heaven is at hand."*
> *Matthew 4:17*

Salvation Is for YOU!

What must you do? You must say sorry for your sins. You must change your attitude and you must start living according to the Word of God and He will make you a new person.

If anyone be in Christ Jesus, he or she is a new creation: *"Therefore, if anyone is in Christ, he is a new creation; old things have passed away; behold, all things have become new"* (2 Corinthians 5:17). All things have passed away and behold, all things have become new. Isn't that wonderful? When God forgives, He forgets.

> *"I, even I, am He who blots out your transgressions for My own sake; and I will not remember your sins.*
> *Isaiah 43:25*

If you are ready to have a changed life, to be forgiven for your sins and to start on a new journey with God, then pray the following prayer:

The Sinner's Prayer

Dear Heavenly Father,

Today I acknowledge that I am a sinner.

Thank You for sending Your Son to die for me on the Cross of Calvary.

By faith I ask You to forgive my sins and to come into my life.

Because of Jesus Christ's death and resurrection all of my sins are forgiven and I am starting a brand-new life today.

In Jesus' name,

Amen.

Name: ______________________________

Date: ______________________________

If you have prayed this prayer, congratulations! You have made the most important decision of your life.

You are starting on an amazing and eternal journey with God. God will walk with you every step of the way. He doesn't promise you there won't be any mountains or any fiery trials, but He does promise you one thing; He says, *"I will never leave you nor forsake you"* (Hebrews 13:5). God bless you.

Now I encourage you to go and tell three people about the wonderful, life-changing decision you have made. Never be ashamed to share this good news!

Therefore, having been justified by faith, we have peace with God through our Lord Jesus Christ.
Romans 5:1

There is therefore now no condemnation to those who are in Christ Jesus.
Romans 8:1

God has given us eternal life, and this life is in His Son. He who has the Son has life; he who does not have the Son of God does not have life. These things I have written to you who believe in the name of the Son of God, that you may know that you have eternal life, and that you may continue to believe in the name of the Son of God.
1 John 5:11-13

The Romans Road

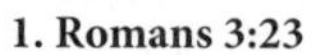

1. Romans 3:23
All have sinned and fall short of the glory of God.

2. Romans 6:23
The wages of sin is death, but the gift of God is eternal life in Christ Jesus our Lord.

3. Romans 5:8
God demonstrates His own love toward us, in that while we were still sinners, Christ died for us.

4. Romans 10:13
For "whoever calls on the name of the Lord shall be saved."

5. Romans 10:9
If you confess with your mouth the Lord Jesus and believe in your heart that God has raised Him from the dead, you will be saved.

6. Romans 8:1
There is therefore now no condemnation to those who are in Christ Jesus.

Assurance of Salvation

Let's take a few moments to recap on what has happened in your life if you have prayed for salvation.

The moment that you received Jesus Christ by faith, many things happened, including the following:

Jesus Christ came into your life

To them God has chosen to make known among the Gentiles the glorious riches of this mystery, which is Christ in you, the hope of glory. Colossians 1:27

Your sins were forgiven

For He has rescued us from the dominion of darkness and brought us into the kingdom of the Son He loves, in whom we have redemption, the forgiveness of sins. Colossians 1:13-14

You became a child of God

Yet to all who did receive Him, to those who believed in His name, He gave the right to become children of God – children born not of natural descent, nor of human decision or a husband's will, but born of God.
John 1:12-13

You received eternal life

"Very truly I tell you, whoever hears My word and believes Him who sent Me has eternal life and will not be judged but has crossed over from death to life." John 5:24

You began the great adventure for which God created you

The thief comes only to steal and kill and destroy; I have come that they may have life, and have it to the full. John 10:10

Isn't it wonderful? Can you think of anything better than having Christ in your life? Pray right now and thank God for the wonderful gift of salvation through His Son, your Saviour and Redeemer, Jesus Christ.

For I am persuaded that neither death nor life, nor angels nor principalities nor powers, nor things present nor things to come, nor height nor depth, nor any other created thing, shall be able to separate us from the love of God which is in Christ Jesus our Lord.
Romans 8:38-39

Don't Rely on Feelings

You might think that you don't feel any different now that you are saved. As a Christian it is important not to be led by feelings that come and go, but by faith in God and the truth contained in His Word. We can rest assured on the absolute certainty of God's Word and not on our own experience.

God's Word and promises are facts we can rely on and form a solid foundation. We base our faith on the firm foundation of truth in God's Word. Our feelings come last and should not control our actions.

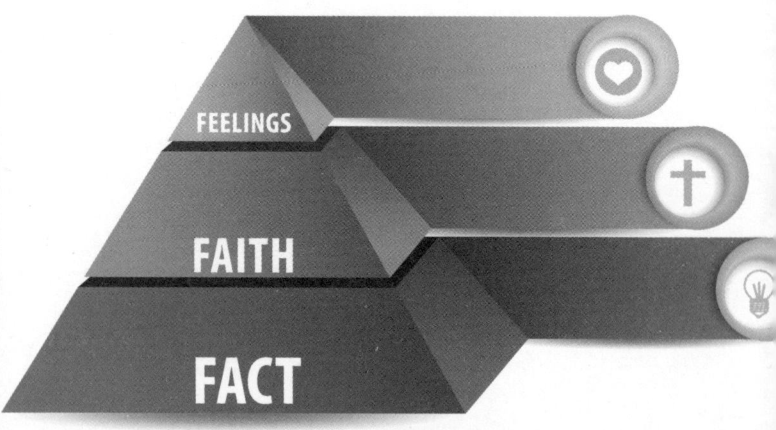

Be on your guard; stand firm
in the faith; be courageous; be strong.
1 Corinthians 16:13

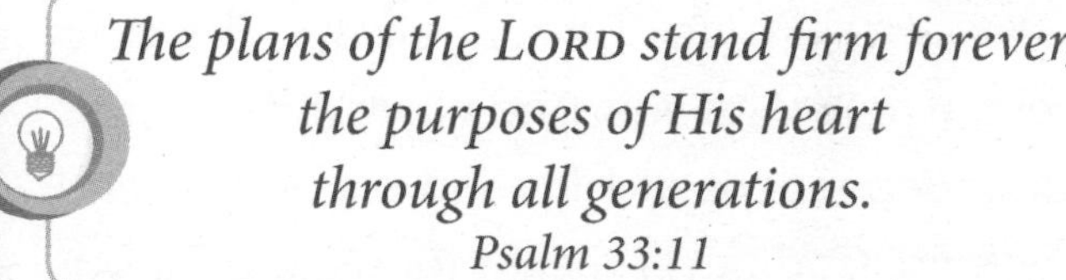

The plans of the Lord stand firm forever,
the purposes of His heart
through all generations.
Psalm 33:11

The grass withers, the flower fades, but
the word of our God stands forever.
Isaiah 40:8

Your word, Lord, is eternal;
it stands firm in the heavens.
Psalm 119:89

My Personal Testimony

I would like to take this opportunity to share my personal testimony with you and to share with you that you never need to travel alone in this life. God is always there to travel the road with you. God never meant for us to be independent of Him and everybody and everything. God never meant for us to do it our way. He meant for us to do it His way because it is the best way.

On 18 February 1979 I reluctantly went to church with my wife. I didn't want to go to church. I wasn't sleeping well, because I owed money and the farm wasn't turning out the way I thought it would and I was under a lot of pressure. I had four little children I had to take care of. I had a labour force, people who were relying on us for money at the end of the month to buy food for their children – I had a responsibility in the district. It all became too much for me. And so I thought that if I went down to the pub or to the country club on a Friday night and had a few ales that it would help me. It did not help me at all. I'd have too many and come home drunk as a coot, as they say. The next morning I would wake up with a hangover. Same problems, same fears, same worries, same responsibilities.

Then Jill, my dear wife and best friend, persuaded me. She said, "Angus, let's go to church." I told her that I didn't really want to go and she replied, "Let's go anyway." We got up early to get ready for church, but we had four children to deal with. By the time we had the whole family ready we were running late, and when we arrived the church was full. The Lord has a real sense of humour: we trooped in and had to walk right up to the front to find seats. Everyone in the congregation knew that Angus Buchan and his family was in church that morning.

"Morning, Farmer!" smiled a friend, and I smiled back. At least I knew somebody.

There was an air of expectancy in the church. The lay people were sharing their testimonies, and I sat there with my mouth open as I listened to them. For the first time in my life I saw strong men cry as they told how the Lord had taken care of their needs, restored their businesses and done wonderful things in their lives.

One man was a building contractor. He started weeping as he told how his business had gone down and he had contemplated suicide. Then he found Jesus, and now he had a reason to live. Another man told how his marriage had been breaking up, when the Lord had brought him and his wife together again. Their stories pierced my heart. For years I had had no interest in religion, but these men's words had a ring of truth. I wanted to be part of this kind of life; I wanted to know more.

"What about you? Would you like to accept Jesus Christ as your Lord and Saviour today?" I looked at the speaker and realised that was exactly what I wanted to do. Jill and I walked to the front of the church with many others, and knelt before the Lord. We prayed the Sinner's Prayer together, saying sorry for our sins and asking Jesus to rule in our hearts, and a miracle happened: Jesus came into our lives.

I knew it was true, though there were no bells ringing, no bright lights, no drama – just a deep assurance in my soul.

In fact, it was only later, as I was walking in the maize fields, that I really understood what had happened. I knew that from now on, Jesus Christ was in total control of my life. No matter what happened, my Lord would take care of everything. Jesus was mine and I was His – forever. An amazing peace came over me, and all my emotional torment, the fear and anxiety and stress fell away. From that moment I called those fields my "green cathedral", the place where I love to walk and talk with my Lord.

> *"Give all your worries and cares to God, for He cares about you."*
> *1 Peter 5:7*

Part 2
GROWING IN GOD

Now that you have accepted Jesus Christ as your Saviour there are a few things we need to discuss as you start the greatest and most important journey of your life. These are things that will help you to grow in your spiritual walk with God.

The Next Step

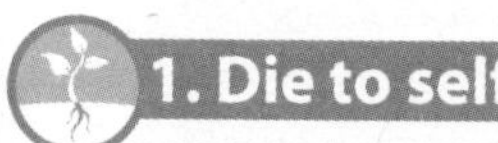

1. Die to self

> You were taught, with regard to your former way of life, to put off your old self, which is being corrupted by its deceitful desires; to be made new in the attitude of your minds; and to put on the new self, created to be like God in true righteousness and holiness.
>
> EPHESIANS 4:22-24

The first thing you must do is to die to self. When you are saved you are born again into a brand-new life and it is time to die to your former life with its sinful desires.

To be born again means to stop the way you are living and to turn around and go the other way. It means new birth. It means a new beginning.

My biggest enemy is not Satan. Satan was defeated when Jesus died on the Cross of Calvary and He rose from the dead three days later. My biggest enemy is self. Flesh. Me. I. No more I – that's how it's got to be with your Christian walk.

Jesus Christ must now be in the driving seat of your life. So stop the car, put the handbrake on, put it into neutral, get out of the car, walk around to the other side and get into the passenger seat. Let Jesus get into the driver's seat. That is growing in God.

If you take a grain of wheat, a maize seed, a sunflower seed, a bean seed, and you just lay it on the road it will never germinate. But if you dig into good fertile soil, you put this seed in there and you cover it up. You know what happens? That seed dies, my friend. It actually rots eventually, but out of it comes new life. That new life will be thirty-, sixty-, one hundred - fold more. But unless that seed dies it stays on its own. That is what growing in God is all about. You must die to self and live for Christ.

The Word of God says, *"Unless a grain of wheat falls into the ground and dies, it remains alone; but if it dies, it produces much grain"* (John 12:24).

Before I became a Christian I was scared to speak to more than two people. If I saw a girl I would run a mile. What happened to me? I died. Jesus Christ came into my heart and I have had the privilege of speaking to hundreds of thousands of people at one meeting. Yes, there has been excitement, there's been a little bit of anxiety, but no fear because the Lord has promised me that He will never leave me and He will never ever forsake me. That is the assurance that I want to give you. You have given your life to Jesus Christ. You've been born again.

You need to forget about yourself, forget about your reputation. It doesn't matter what people say about you. That is why I always say that once you have prayed the Sinner's Prayer, go and find the first three people that you can and tell them what you have done. Tell them that you have given your life to Jesus Christ.

I have been crucified with Christ; it is no longer I who live, but Christ lives in me; and the life which I now live in the flesh I live by faith in the Son of God, who loved me and gave Himself for me.
Galatians 2:20

Therefore, if anyone is in Christ, the new creation has come: The old has gone, the new is here!
2 Corinthians 5:17

Those who belong to Christ Jesus have crucified the flesh with its passions and desires.
Galatians 5:24

2. Pick up your cross and follow Jesus

Jesus says that unless a man denies himself, takes up his cross and follows Him daily, he cannot be His disciple.

When we are born again we are no longer slaves to sin, but become followers of Jesus who is our Lord and Master. We no longer live for ourselves, but for Him. We obey Him and do what He wants us to. This is not always an easy road to follow, but it is the best one. This is the road that leads to holiness.

Holiness is the end product of obedience. When you become an obedient man or woman, you become a holy man or woman. We need to walk the walk of holiness.

If you have a short temper, it's got to stop. You can't tell me you love Jesus and you're screaming and shouting at everybody. It's got to change. That is selfishness. It's got to stop.

*Then Jesus said to His disciples,
"Whoever wants to be My disciple must deny themselves and take up their cross and follow Me. For whoever wants to save their life will lose it, but whoever loses their life for Me will find it."*
Matthew 16:24-25

*Then He said to them all,
"If anyone desires to come after Me, let him deny himself, and take up his cross daily, and follow Me."*
Luke 9:23

"And whoever does not carry their cross and follow Me cannot be My disciple."
Luke 14:27

When you start on your new journey of following Jesus you might find that you are tempted to go back to old sinful habits. You need to resist temptation and ask God to help you to obey Him. He will strengthen you and help you to stand strong against temptation. He will never let you be tempted beyond what you can bear.

If you do sin, don't give up. Ask God to forgive you. God is merciful and kind and knows your heart. If you repent and ask His forgiveness, He will forgive you.

Growing in God is all about how we live. There is no other way that I can live or want to live. And it's exciting. And it is full of joy.

No temptation has overtaken you except what is common to mankind. And God is faithful; He will not let you be tempted beyond what you can bear. But when you are tempted, He will also provide a way out so that you can endure it.
1 Corinthians 10:13

I can do all things through Christ who gives me strength.
Philippians 4:13

3. Join a church

Once you start on your new journey of following Jesus, you need to join a fellowship of believers.

John Wesley, one of the greatest evangelists who ever lived, said that if you take a coal out of the fire and you put it by itself it will die. We need each other. You need to get involved in a church that worships God and teaches the Bible. You need to share with others who know God and have dedicated their lives to Him.

And let us consider how we may spur one
another on toward love and good deeds,
not giving up meeting together,
as some are in the habit of doing,
but encouraging one another – and all
the more as you see the Day approaching.
Hebrews 10:24-25

They devoted themselves to the apostles' teaching and to fellowship, to the breaking of bread and to prayer. Everyone was filled with awe at the many wonders and signs performed by the apostles. All the believers were together and had everything in common. They sold property and possessions to give to anyone who had need. Every day they continued to meet together in the temple courts. They broke bread in their homes and ate together with glad and sincere hearts, praising God and enjoying the favor of all the people. And the Lord added to their number daily those who were being saved.

Acts 2:42-47

4. Be baptised

Baptism is another step in your journey with the Lord. You need to be baptised in water. Why? Because it is a statement that you are making to the world. The old man has died, the new man is alive.

The Bible compares our immersion into water with the death of Jesus Christ and the death of our old self, and as we come up out of the water we are symbolically washed clean and raised up to a new life just as Jesus was raised up from the dead.

Peter replied, "Repent and
be baptized, every one of you,
in the name of Jesus Christ for
the forgiveness of your sins.
And you will receive the gift
of the Holy Spirit.
Acts 2:38

Or don't you know that all of us who were baptized into Christ Jesus were baptized into His death? We were therefore buried with Him through baptism into death in order that, just as Christ was raised from the dead through the glory of the Father, we too may live a new life. For if we have been united with Him in a death like His, we will certainly also be united with Him in a resurrection like His.

Romans 6:3-5

Therefore go and make disciples of all nations, baptizing them in the name of the Father and of the Son and of the Holy Spirit.

Matthew 28:19

Aids for Your Spiritual Journey

1. Walk in the power of the Holy Spirit

The Holy Spirit is known as the Helper and the Comforter. He dwells inside those who have given their lives to Christ. When you have the Holy Spirit in your life you are empowered to live the Christian life and you have the strength to continue on your journey.

The Holy Spirit dwells in you

Do you not know that you are the temple of God and that the Spirit of God dwells in you? If anyone defiles the temple of God, God will destroy him. For the temple of God is holy, which temple you are. 1 Corinthians 3:16-17

Now the one who has fashioned us for this very purpose is God, who has given us the Spirit as a deposit, guaranteeing what is to come. 2 Corinthians 5:5

God's love has been poured out into our hearts through the Holy Spirit, who has been given to us. Romans 5:5

The Holy Spirit is your helper

"And I will pray the Father, and He will give you another Helper, that He may abide with you forever – the Spirit of truth, whom the world cannot receive, because it neither sees Him nor knows Him; but you know Him, for He dwells with you and will be in you." John 14:16-17

"But the Helper, the Holy Spirit, whom the Father will send in My name, He will teach you all things, and bring to your remembrance all things that I said to you." John 14:26

"However, when He, the Spirit of truth, has come, He will guide you into all truth; for He will not speak on His own authority, but whatever He hears He will speak; and He will tell you things to come." John 16:13

Likewise the Spirit also helps in our weaknesses. For we do not know what we should pray for as we ought, but the Spirit Himself makes intercession for us with groanings which cannot be uttered. Romans 8:26

2. Prayer is your lifeline

I cannot face the day without first spending time with the Master. As an evangelist, I speak about Him and to Him all the time, but I also need an intimate, one-on-one time with Him. It is like spending time with your spouse – when you are with them at a social gathering, it's wonderful because your spouse is with you, but there has to be a time when it is just the two of you.

That intimacy is so important for a successful marriage and so it is in our walk with the Lord. If there is no intimacy – no special relationship – then it will not last.

As a new believer I was taught a simple method of praying using the acronym ACTS which I will share with you on the following pages. This is a great way to pray.

Make prayer time a special time each day and be sure to share with the Lord everything that is on your heart and that is happening in your life.

A stands for **A**doration. This is the time to adore the Lord for who He is, to give Him thanks for a new day; to praise Him that you are alive, that your family is alive, that it is a beautiful new morning. There are so many things to praise Him for – the promise that He will never leave us nor forsake us; the fact that He is the same yesterday, today and forever.

C stands for **C**onfession. This is the time to repent before the Lord, to ask God to forgive your sins. Maybe you lost your temper with your family unintentionally; maybe it's something you've neglected to do; maybe you have offended the Lord in some area. Ask forgiveness and the Lord will forgive you. He says in 1 John 1:9: *"If we confess our sins, He is faithful and just to forgive us our sins and to cleanse us from all unrighteousness."*

stands for **T**hanksgiving. We should thank God that our names are written in the Lamb's Book of Life. It doesn't matter how hard we work. It's not about that – it's about His grace, His undeserved loving kindness that gives us the opportunity to call ourselves His children. We can thank Him for our family and loved ones; for new opportunities in life. There are so many things to be grateful for.

stands for **S**upplication. Pray for your loved ones and yourself. Bring all your requests before God concerning your life and your family's well-being and future. Pray specifically, expectantly and faithfully.

Now this is the confidence that we have in Him, that if we ask anything according to His will, He hears us. And if we know that He hears us, whatever we ask, we know that we have the petitions that we have asked of Him.

1 John 5:14-15

Be anxious for nothing, but in everything by prayer and supplication, with thanksgiving, let your requests be made known to God; and the peace of God, which surpasses all understanding, will guard your hearts and minds through Christ Jesus.

Philippians 4:6-7

Rejoice always, pray without ceasing, in everything give thanks; for this is the will of God in Christ Jesus for you.

1 Thessalonians 5:16-18

"Call upon Me in the day of trouble; I will deliver you, and you shall glorify Me."

Psalm 50:15

3. The Bible is your compass

Psalm 119:105 says, *"Your Word is a lamp to my feet and a light to my path."* And that is why I love this Book so much. You have no idea how much the Bible means to me. The older I get the more I realise that everything you need to know about is in the Bible.

God's Word is still the all-time best-seller. There is no other book in the world that sells more copies than the Bible. There are millions of copies of the Bible being given away every day in many languages all over the world and it is still called The Good News.

> Jesus answered, "It is written: 'Man shall not live on bread alone, but on every word that comes from the mouth of God.'"
>
> Matthew 4:4

It is the Bread of Life. You see, it never gets old, it never gets stale. It is relevant to all of us. And I want to tell you it is the best guidance and help we have on our spiritual journey.

Everything that God has put in this Book applies to you and me, but you see, you've got to spend time reading the Book in order to understand it. Daily reading of the Bible is crucial to your spiritual journey. The Bible acts as your compass as it guides and leads you. There is so much to learn from God's holy Word.

You might wonder where to start, so I will explain how I read the Bible. I do not believe in just opening the Bible at any place and putting your finger on a verse and hoping for the best. I read the Bible systematically every single day. I have a notebook and everything that God tells me through the Scripture I write down. For example, I'll start in the Psalms (the Old Testament) and then I'll start in the New Testament in the Gospel of John, because it's nice and easy reading and very encouraging. I will read a portion every day; some days I will read a chapter, some days it might be ten verses. I will read it maybe more than once and then write down in my quiet time book – a diary or journal – what the Lord has said to me that day. I am a slow learner, but when I write something down, I remember it.

All Scripture is God-breathed and is useful for teaching, rebuking, correcting and training in righteousness, so that the servant of God may be thoroughly equipped for every good work.
2 Timothy 3:16-17

Keep this Book of the Law always on your lips; meditate on it day and night, so that you may be careful to do everything written in it. Then you will be prosperous and successful.
Joshua 1:8

For the word of God is alive and active. Sharper than any double-edged sword, it penetrates even to dividing soul and spirit, joints and marrow; it judges the thoughts and attitudes of the heart.
Hebrews 4:12

I seek You with all my heart;
do not let me stray from Your commands.
I have hidden Your word in my heart
that I might not sin against You.
Psalm 119:10-11

Like newborn babies, crave pure spiritual milk, so that by it you may grow up in your salvation, now that you have tasted that the Lord is good.
1 Peter 2:2-3

The law of the LORD is perfect, converting the soul; the testimony of the LORD is sure, making wise the simple; the statutes of the LORD are right, rejoicing the heart; the commandment of the LORD is pure, enlightening the eyes; the fear of the LORD is clean, enduring forever; the judgments of the LORD are true and righteous altogether. More to be desired are they than gold, yea, than much fine gold; sweeter also than honey and the honeycomb. Moreover by them Your servant is warned, and in keeping them there is great reward.
Psalm 19:7-11

Part 3
THE GREAT COMMISSION

Then the eleven disciples went away into Galilee, to the mountain which Jesus had appointed for them. When they saw Him, they worshiped Him; but some doubted. And Jesus came and spoke to them, saying, "All authority has been given to Me in heaven and on earth. Go therefore and make disciples of all the nations, baptizing them in the name of the Father and of the Son and of the Holy Spirit, teaching them to observe all things that I have commanded you; and lo, I am with you always, even to the end of the age. Amen."

Matthew 28:16-20

In this third and final section of *Starting the Journey*, I want to speak to you about a high and holy calling that our Saviour has given to every one of us who believe in Him.

As believers we can't sit back and keep the wonderful, life-changing news of salvation to ourselves. We need to go and tell others about what we have found.

Before departing from the disciples and descending into heaven, Jesus gave them one final instruction. He told the disciples to "Go and make disciples of all the nations". This is the Great Commission and is addressed to every believer in Christ.

Sharing the Good News with others around you

> "You will receive power when the Holy Spirit comes on you; and you will be My witnesses in Jerusalem, and in all Judea and Samaria, and to the ends of the earth."
> ACTS 1:8

The Great Commission is telling others what Jesus has done for you. And that is what you and I need to do. We need to go into all the world and preach the gospel. Where do we start? Do we start at the outer ends of the world and work our way in? No. We start in Jerusalem. Where is Jerusalem? It's in your home. It's with your spouse and your children. With your parents, relatives and friends. First Jerusalem, then Judea, then Samaria and then the outer ends of the world.

Spending time with Jesus is the best preparation for telling others the Good News

You cannot go and tell other people how to live their lives when you yourself have not walked the road. But this doesn't mean that you have to wait till you have been a Christian for your whole life. Some of the greatest preachers who have ever lived finished their ministry before they were even 30 years old. I am thinking particularly of Jim Elliott; he was 28 years old when he was killed in the Amazon jungle preaching the gospel. I think of Robert Murray M'Cheyne who was 29 years old when he died, preaching the gospel. God used him to start that huge revival in Dundee, Scotland.

The Master Himself lived on earth for only 33 years. So it is not about age. It is about spending time with God. Jesus spent much time with God and He is my role model and I am sure you will find Him to be the best role model too.

Many a time the disciples had the crowd waiting on the shores of Lake Galilee. Where was the Master? No one could find Him. He was up in the hills, hearing from His Father, spending time with God.

Come away. Come away, my beloved. Come away and rest. You need to take time out to get to know God and His will.

Be a clay vessel in the hands of the Lord

> We have this treasure in jars of clay to show that this all-surpassing power is from God and not from us.
>
> 2 Corinthians 4:7

We need to remember that it is God who brings a man to salvation. We are the messengers, the clay vessels that He uses to spread the message of salvation. We tell others about Him, but He works in their hearts.

As messengers of the Good News, we need to spend time with God. We need to hear from God so that when He calls us, we can speak. The best way we can prepare ourselves to be vessels for Him is to spend time in prayer and the Word. I want to encourage you to start memorizing Scripture. Jesus quoted Scripture all the time because He is the Word. And you need to memorise the Word of God if you want to become a messenger of the Good News.

In order to help you in this very fruitful and beneficial habit of Scripture memorisation, I have included a starter list of Scriptures to memorise at the end of this book.

Not all of us are called to be preachers; some of us are called to be housewives, some of us are called to be school teachers, some are called to be professional sportsmen. Others are called to be farmers. But in it all the Great Commission takes place.

Remember the eleven men who took the gospel into all the world. What were they? They were fishermen, they were businessmen, they were normal men who came from every walk of life. And that is the Good News. People want to know about things that are relevant to them. They don't want to hear about pie in the sky. They want to know what to do when they have a sick child in the family. What to do when the debt collector knocks at their door. What to do when they have messed up and want to start again. That, my friend, is when you can tell them about your life-changing experience.

You don't have to go to Bible school to be a witness

You don't have to wait till you think you are holy and perfect before you start sharing the Gospel. Not at all. In fact the older you get the more you realise what a sinner you actually are and it's only by the grace of God that you'll make it. It's like looking at yourself in a mirror with a bright light shining down. The closer you get to the light the more you start seeing all the dirt in the pores of your skin. The closer you get to Jesus, the more you realise how unworthy you are.

You don't first need to go to theological seminary before you tell others about Christ. Those years that I spent in the field sowing and ploughing were years that the Lord taught me about Himself. The same thing happened to Saul. Saul of Tarsus (who became Paul, the great apostle) didn't go to a seminary in Jerusalem. He was sent to Arabia. He was sent there for 13 years. Nobody even knew about him. God taught him. The disciples themselves were unlearned men, but they had walked with Jesus.

Prayer is a form of witness

If somebody says they are feeling sick or they have a problem, pray for them yourself. There is great power in prayer. You don't need to call a pastor, you can pray for them. In the workplace, wherever you are. From personal experience I can say that it is wonderful when a man comes to look at my cattle, and we have a chat over tea afterwards and I ask him how he's doing. All of a sudden the man breaks down and starts to weep. He says that his wife has left him or he's just heard that a family member is very sick. Then I ask if I can pray for him. In such situations the answer is always "Yes, please." Do you know that I have never had a man refuse prayer? I am talking about a Hindu man, a Muslim man, an atheist, a backslider.

When I do hospital visitations, I take my Bible with me and they let me right into the ICU. And often I'll be praying for a person in one bed and before I leave I look across and I see somebody just lying there and I say, "Sir/Madam, may I pray for you?" They always say yes.

Counting the Cost

It's a privilege and an honour to be known as an ambassador of Jesus Christ and you can be one too. God has called us to go into all the world and to preach the gospel to every creature. But you might be called to pay a price. I am paying my price at the moment.

The first campaign I ever had was in Ladysmith in 1989. God asked me three questions driving into that town: Are you prepared to be a fool for Me? Are you prepared for people to say all manner of evil about you for My name's sake? And the hardest one, are you prepared to see less of your family for My name's sake? And I said, Lord, only by Your grace, I'll drink of the cup. I don't sleep in my own bed very often anymore. And remember, for a farmer that is most unusual, but it's a small price to pay when I think of what Jesus did for me.

So go out into all the world and preach the gospel. I am praying for you for boldness and for courage and for compassion for the lost.

If you have been born again and
have started on your journey with God,
Angus would love to hear from you.

Please feel free to contact him:

angus@angusbuchan.co.za

PO Box 373, Greytown, 3250, KZN, RSA

or the publisher at:

copy@cum.co.za

Put on the Armour of God

Ephesians 6:10-18

Easy Scripture Reference Guide

The Bible is your compass and the Scripture verses in this section will serve to steer you as you navigate your course on your journey through life.

Where to find it in the Bible

The Ten Commandments – Exodus 20:1-17

The Lord Is My Shepherd – Psalm 23

Jesus Christ's Birth – Matthew 1:18-2:15

The Beatitudes – Matthew 5:3-12

The Lord's Prayer – Matthew 6:5-15

The Greatest Commandment – Matthew 22:34-40

The Crucifixion & Resurrection – Matthew 26-28

Believers as One Body – 1 Corinthians 12:12-31

The Chapter on Love – 1 Corinthians 13

Starting to Memorise Scripture

Scripture memorisation is a powerful tool in your Christian walk. These Scriptures form the foundation of your faith and will remain with you throughout your life. They will also give you encouragement and direction when you need it. So start today and store God's Word in your heart!

Scripture Verses about Salvation

John 3:16

For God so loved the world that He gave His one and only Son, that whoever believes in Him shall not perish but have eternal life.

John 14:6

Jesus answered, "I am the way and the truth and the life. No one comes to the Father except through Me."

Romans 5:8

But God demonstrates His own love for us in this: While we were still sinners, Christ died for us.

Romans 8:28

And we know that in all things God works for the good of those who love Him, who have been called according to His purpose.

Romans 3:23-24

For all have sinned and fall short of the glory of God, and all are justified freely by His grace through the redemption that came by Christ Jesus.

Galatians 2:20

I have been crucified with Christ and I no longer live, but Christ lives in me. The life I live in the body, I live by faith in the Son of God, who loved me and gave Himself for me.

Ephesians 2:8-9

For it is by grace you have been saved, through faith – and this not from yourselves, it is the gift of God – not by works, so that no one can boast.

Isaiah 53:5

But He was pierced for our transgressions, He was crushed for our iniquities; the punishment that brought us peace was upon Him, and by His wounds we are healed.

1 John 1:9

If we confess our sins, He is faithful and just and will forgive us our sins and purify us from all unrighteousness.

Scripture Verses on Living the Christian Life

Galatians 5:22-24

But the fruit of the Spirit is love, joy, peace, patience, kindness, goodness, faithfulness, gentleness and self-control. Against such things there is no law. Those who belong to Christ Jesus have crucified the sinful nature with its passions and desires.

Joshua 1:9

Have I not commanded you? Be strong and courageous. Do not be terrified; do not be discouraged, for the LORD your God will be with you wherever you go.

Proverbs 3:5-6

Trust in the LORD with all your heart and lean not on your own understanding; in all your ways acknowledge Him, and he will make your paths straight.

Isaiah 40:30-31

Even youths grow tired and weary, and young men stumble and fall; but those who hope in the LORD will renew their strength. They will soar on wings like eagles; they will run and not grow weary, they will walk and not be faint.

Jeremiah 29:11

"For I know the plans I have for you," declares the LORD, "plans to prosper you and not to harm you, plans to give you hope and a future."

Philippians 4:8

Finally, brothers, whatever is true, whatever is noble, whatever is right, whatever is pure, whatever is lovely, whatever is admirable – if anything is excellent or praiseworthy – think about such things.

Philippians 4:13

I can do everything through Him who gives me strength.

Romans 12:2

Do not conform any longer to the pattern of this world, but be transformed by the renewing of your mind. Then you will be able to test and approve what God's will is – His good, pleasing and perfect will.

Philippians 4:5-7

Let your gentleness be evident to all. The Lord is near. Do not be anxious about anything, but in everything, by prayer and petition, with thanksgiving, present your requests to God. And the peace of God, which transcends all understanding, will guard your hearts and your minds in Christ Jesus.

Psalm 18:30

God's way is perfect. All the LORD's promises prove true. He is a shield for all who look to Him for protection.

Have mercy upon me, O God,
according to Your lovingkindness;
according to the multitude
of Your tender mercies,
blot out my transgressions.
Wash me thoroughly from my iniquity,
and cleanse me from my sin.
Purge me with hyssop, and I shall be clean;
wash me, and I shall be whiter than snow.
Create in me a clean heart, O God,
and renew a steadfast spirit within me.
Do not cast me away from Your presence,
and do not take Your Holy Spirit from me.
Restore to me the joy of Your salvation,
and uphold me by Your generous Spirit.

Psalm 51:1-2, 7, 10-12

DAVID'S PRAYER OF CONFESSION AND REPENTANCE